DISCARD

POEMS

of

DANIEL WHITEHEAD HICKY

Atlanta

Cherokee Publishing Company

1975

Library of Congress Catalog Card Number: 75-16360
ISBN: 0-87797-032-7

Copies of *Poems of Daniel Whitehead Hicky* may be
obtained through leading booksellers or by writing direct to
Cherokee Publishing Company's sales office: P.O. Box 1081,
Covington, Georgia 30209. Send $6.95 plus 25¢ handling
charge. Georgia residents add 21¢ sales tax and, where
applicable, 7¢ MARTA tax.

PRINTED IN THE UNITED STATES OF AMERICA

Acknowledgement

The author expresses appreciation for permission to include in this volume certain of his poems which first appeared in the pages of *Harper's Magazine, The Saturday Review of Literature, Scribner's Magazine, The American Mercury, Harper's Bazaar, The Saturday Evening Post, Cosmopolitan Magazine, The New York Times, McCall's Magazine, The Catholic World, The Ladies' Home Journal, The North American Review, The Georgia Review, New York Herald-Tribune, Good Housekeeping, The Yale Review, Georgia Magazine,* and *The Progressive Farmer.*

Volumes of Poetry
By Daniel Whitehead Hicky

POEMS
WILD HERON
BRIGHT HARBOR
CALL BACK THE SPRING
NEVER THE NIGHTINGALE
THIRTEEN SONNETS OF GEORGIA

CONTENTS

POEMS OF
DANIEL WHITEHEAD HICKY

THE IVORY TOWER

So long my heart has sickened of the noise
Of cities when they lie awake, or sleep,
Men chattering like sparrows in self-praise,
Recounting all the worldly goods they reap,
I shall go back and seek the ivory tower,
The door I have forsaken, find the key,
And light the logs again and watch the hour
Drift like a leaf relinquished quietly.
I shall be then not lonely as I am
Treading the busy streets half-mad, half-blind,
Among all men a poet set apart.
I shall relearn all I have lost to them
Searching the secret jungles of the heart,
The pale moon-drenched himalayas of the mind.

ALWAYS, ALWAYS

ALWAYS, always, it will be thus: the sun
Unfolded like a blinding marigold,
The bright noon's fiery embers swiftly done
And twilight scattering shadows blue and cold.
April upon the bough and all too brief,
The ripened fruit, and leaves that bleed and burn,
Young lovers with their passions and their grief,
Age hoarding dreams like petals in an urn.
Always, always, it has been thus since Time
Unloosed the emerald rhythms of the sea,
Since first the white-winged moon began to climb
The waiting night. Beloved, and what are we
But lesser than the quiver of a flower,
We with our little words, our little hour?

I HAVE A NEED OF GULLS

I have a need of gulls again and their flying
Over the foam-white acres of the sea
Where the sunrise drifts like a fleet of ships afire,
And the dark like eternity.
I have a need for the yellow sea oat's music
And the single salty note
Curled in the palm of a shell as pale as the sigh
In a sandpiper's throat.

Too long the city has housed me and fed me its fare,
Too long I have run with the crowd;
I have a need to be free again like the gulls,
To bathe my face in the cool white peace of a cloud.
I have a need to lie at length on the sands,
To unshoulder my burdens out where the seagulls cry,
And to all of my heart's dark questions unanswered
Hear the white answers they write in the sky.

THE RETURN

IT was a fitting time to come back home.
Too long my feet had wandered, and the years
Like weeds had grown between us, shoulder-high.
I saw it from the hilltop, saw through tears
My long lost childhood in the apple boughs,
And greening underneath that stretch of sky
A willow I had planted beside the house.
Now I was turning home, and I had come
A long, long way through Time, was back again
With all my heart had lost. The farm lay there
Waiting in sunlight for me. All was plain
Once more, nothing was lost, O nothing now!
I quickened my steps and suddenly, I declare,
Before I reached the quiet hilltop's brow
The apple trees came running half the way,
And as I met them shamefully face to face
They reached out blossoming boughs that sun-drenched day
And swung me up in their forgiving embrace.

SUMMERTIME HILL

IT is summer now, the half-awakened hour for bee and clover,
For yellow butterflies in the cannas' scarlet throats,
Summer, when still the breath of the shattering lilac lingers
And the slow incense of the moonflower lifts and floats.

He lies asleep, or on the green edges of sleep, this boy
With a dozen small summers behind him, forgot like a prayer,
His cap pulled over his nose to lessen the freckles.
The sun and the sweat of the day have captured his hair.

Far up in the oceans of sky his ships are sailing,
The pale and the lean flotillas of cloud and space;
Beside him a hornet explores the lashes of a daisy's eye,
The wind blows hot through a pattern of Queen Anne's lace.

Still he sleeps away the summer's luxurious hour.
Her secret, sun-bright kiss on his lips as he lies
Silent as the slumbering passions within his veins,
As the blue, unspoken thunder in his eyes.

FOR MORE THAN BEAUTY

FOR more than beauty have I need:
The stirring earth, the bursting seed
That lifts slow fire into the air,
Perfume like incense rising clear
Where laurel takes a mountainside,
The thunder of a moon-washed tide
Against the darkness of a reef—
These shall not appease my grief.

Beauty can fill the sky with light,
But not the empty heart when night
Has strung a million stars above.
She cannot fuel the lamp of love
Nor set it bright upon the sill;
She never has; she never will.
And cold she lies, as cold as stone
Against his heart who sleeps alone.

CHILD WATCHING A SNAIL

WITHIN the garden's close embrace, secure
As though it were a world for you alone,
I watch you ponder on the slow and sure
Pathway a lone snail journeys to a stone.
It takes an hour you say to pass a rose
Kindling its fire beside the walk; a day
To reach a gate the wind will never close;
Nothing can quicken its slow, unhurried way.
O child bewildered in the summer sun,
Too swiftly, all too swiftly, all things pass:
Bright stars at dusk, the evening's moon, half-blown,
Love, even love, like shadows on the grass.
Censure it not, this snail with silver glow;
Across your heart may Time move half as slow.

WAR HAS ITS DAY

WAR has its day. Each generation knows
   The stricken field, the city sacked by fire,
Its crawling refugees, the child that goes
   With shrapnel-lighted eyes from pyre to pyre;
Cathedrals packed with worshipers too late
   To summon God above the battles' thunder;
No sea but in due time has borne the weight
   Of blood upon its waters, men sucked under.
So it has always been. But, warring done,
   Child that he is, man will return at last
Shame-faced and prodigal, and once again
   As though at some new wonder from the East,
Bewildered, stare upon a sparrow's wing,
   A snowdrop pressing at the heart of spring.

THIS HAVE I LEARNED

THIS have I learned in the ways of the world:
Whether on Singapore's street
Or a crooked lane where the Casbah runs,
To the lips a melon is sweet.

Grief is the same and as fathomless,
Knife-turning is its cry;
On Labrador's ice or a hillside in Spain
Death stares as cold from each eye.

And love is the world's red rose wherever
To the weary and old without sight
No less than deep in the hearts of the lads.
This I remember tonight.

BRIEF FAREWELL

STRANGE how we met, and laughed, and said small words
Deep in the busy street, then journeyed on,
A farewell casual as the flight of birds
From spring-white boughs, or darkness from the dawn.
There was so much to say above the crowd,
So much for eye to eye, for hand to hand
To tell by look, or touch, and yet we stood
Speechless as aliens in an alien land.
I might have told you how the long days reach
Like tideless seas across the heart and mind,
How letters once you wrote lie each to each,
Read and re-read when twilight draws the blind,
Yet in a moment's space you waved goodbye,
Lost in a city not needing you as I.

BOY IN SPRING

THIS is the tremulous time of year
A boy will pause and suddenly stare
Into the fire a flower makes,
Tracing the dark, the lighter streaks,
Within his quick hands, bit by bit,
Or in his mind unraveling it.
And he will throw his book aside,
Faun that he is, and leap and hide
Where maple branches open wide
To let him ambush in their cove
Of cool green leaves, green skies above,
And be the first, or almost so,
To watch the birds come back, to know
Upon what bough, beneath what leaf
They build their little house of grief.
And he will lie upon the grass
For hours to watch a lizard pass,
Or catch a firefly, almost shout
To see its yellow light go out.

Spring is the only time a boy
Can let his heart overrun with joy.
Autumn is not for him, the cold
November days of drifted gold,

Nor winter coming fast upon
The birches turning red to brown.
The year is going then, is gone,
Darkness without, and dark within.
A boy must be where things begin,
His ears attuned, sharp as a knife,
Pressed close upon the heart of life.

THE DAY YOU DIE

THE day you die I will not come and say:
Poor weary dust, how rested now, at peace,
Nor shed a tear upon that bitter day
Above the new turned earth granting you release.
I will go seeking all you were and find
Dark eyes that I remember where larkspurs blow,
And, listening, pluck your voice from the warm wind
As clearly as a red rose from the snow.
Granite can never capture nor hold you fast;
Forever at my side your steps shall be,
Tracing the paths we knew and loved the best,
And searching restless patterns of the sea
I will find your face in all the tides that run,
Your laughter, defiant, lifting toward the sun.

LINES FOR A SUMMER DAY

THE world is yours today, my lad. Your feet
Possess each mile of daisy fields they cover,
And where they pause beside the cool retreat
Of shady brooks and hillsides red with clover,
They, too, are yours, and all the butterflies
You chase like shining arrows down the wind,
The robins in the willows, and the skies
Bluer than seas of larkspur. You will find
The wildflowers ring their bells for you; the grass
Grows sweet beneath your shadow as you run,
And all the furry fellows as you pass
Will pause to greet you in the summer sun.
Remember, as the twilight takes the lane,
The world is yours today, but never again.

HYACINTHS

You brought me hyacinths when there was no spring,
And snow lay like a white prayer on the world.
Warm blue they were, the color of seas that sing
Small broken songs when sunlit tides are curled
With all the passion of a lover's hands,
And I could read deep in your eyes of gray
The silent thundering love understands,
And all the shining words you could not say.
Others have brought me light within their eyes,
Others have lain their hands upon mine here,
But with your hyacinths there blossomed skies
Where no cloud was, and sunlight shimmered clear.
Pressed now within a book these hyacinths hold
The love you brought me from the blinding cold.

WORDS FOR A RISING MOON

I cannot say what lovers side by side
Slumber beneath hot stars in Singapore,
With velvet-scented fingers to explore,
What darkened Arab turns him to his bride
In silken tents spread on the desert's floor,
Nor in their year of ice what Viking's fire
Burns through the night in torrents of desire.

But love, beside me under this same moon
We are as one, all lovers in the night;
Whether we speak our words by jungle light,
By flashing scimitars or eerie tune
Of ivory horn, when moons hang yellow and bright
We turn, and each to each, Nome to Cape Town—
In love's fierce tide we drift, and drifting, drown.

SONNET

WHEN you and I have grown too old for loving
   The first slow tide of dawn across the dark,
Too old to pause, bewildered, when a lark
   Plunges its arrow of music where we are roving;
When the first rose of April fails to quicken
   Our pulse and hold us speechless for a spell,
And we are tired, too tired to sit and tell
   Love's words again, and watch the bright stars thicken,—
When comes that hour and the spirit sighs,
   Though still we talk as one who understands,
Feel summer's sunlight and the winter's knife,
   Ah, little do we know that all of life
Will lie upon a bier with folded hands
   And silent lips, and pennies on its eyes.

SILENCE

MAN'S eager mind, his cunning hand
Have shaped no thing in all the land
That rises as a shadow might,
Assumes a certain form and height,
But in its smallest motion even
Shatters all silence under heaven.
Building a tower that will last
Only until his day is past,
In struggling up or swinging down
Above the gaping of the town,
His derricks and his engines' roar
Will thunder for a mile or more.

From silence man has much to learn:
How frailest lamps that fireflies burn
Flash on and off and off and on
As silently as winds at dawn;
How lonely pines attain the sky
With less than any needle's sigh,
Attaining it, give back again
A forest thick as sudden rain;
Earth turning slowly, dark to light,
As quietly as a feather's flight.

Some day, perhaps, with war laid by,
In brothership, seeing eye to eye,
When armies of the world shall till
The ravished field, the blackened hill,
God will return to earth again,
Peace falling like sunlight over grain,
And calling men from every land,
Divulge the secrets of His hand.

Then shall we hear, with ears attuned,
The cool blue turbines of the wind,
The generators of the sea,
Their foam-white rhythms quietly
Drawing the silver of a tide,
Shaping its pattern far and wide;
Where April suddenly breaks and flows,
The scarlet diesels of the rose.

LOST: A CHILDHOOD

HAS anyone seen a little boy running
As fast as a colt I would say,
Past hedges of months, past thickets of years,
Running forever away?
His face was all freckles,
His hands bore the fragrance
Of all that was green in the spring.
Did he run past the gate
Or trample your meadow
As swift as an arrow shot from a sling?
Think hard, lest I never
And never shall find him,
His lips like wild strawberries,
His blue eyes aflame—
Did you hear him or see him
And O, if you did,
Did he pause there and, breathless,
Answer my name?

THE LONELY OLD MEN

Now through the lavender silences of duskfall
The old men go their lonely shadowy way
Along the lighting streets and country roads,
Beside the razored wind-drifts of the bay.

I speak for them who will not turn tonight
The well-worn knobs of any remembered door,
Being lost and outside Time, being left like leaves
Trembling and pushed aside by the traffic's roar.

With every dusk you may see them, the old men going
Nowhere like shadows when the earliest lamplight gleams,
Needing across the night, as dark as its moon,
An ember of brothership, a crust of dreams.

IRISH ELEGY

LITTLE it was, O little it was
She ever asked of me:
A roof against the darkening rain,
A spot of bread and tea,
And understanding, tenderness
Somewhere from dark till dawn—
O that was all she begged of me,
My love that now is gone.

And I, what did I ask of her,
In looking back today?
The first red rose of every spring,
Words brushing sorrow away,
More love than any woman can give,
Balm healing all my scars—
O yes, and I the greedy one,
The sun and a scatter of stars.

I HAVE A NEED OF YOU

I have a need of you such as the night
For silence and the fiery Pleiades,
Such as my room has need of candlelight
And hearthlogs when the dark wind bows the trees.
You are a part of me, as much a part
As petals are a part of any flower;
You are the heartbeats ringing in my heart,
The minutes chiming away each shining hour.
No stars drift outward on the tides of dawn,
No suns like burning ships go down the west,
But your dark hair across my pillow is thrown
Softer than moonlight, and my lips are pressed
Upon your lips. Ah love, with every breath
I have a need of you, past even death.

ONLY THE LIVING

O not the dead left on the fields of battle,
The dying with last daylight in their eye
Can know again the taste of death, its rattle
Like gunfire down a red astonished sky.
Only the living who return at last
Limping upon the arm of Time can know
The death that is forever, that will blast
Beauty from April's blossom, winter's snow.
They must sit out and sun their years away
Staring at shattered feet that raced the wind,
At shrunken arms that held the world one day,
Hearing the choking throat, the broken mind,
Cursing their God, the fumbling shell that gave
Their youth this long slow conference with the grave.

A LOVER'S PRAYER

FASHION no rose, O Lord, as sweet as lips
   That I have known tonight,
No petals softer than her fingertips,
   No star as bright
As eyes that hold me in their burning spell;
   Fashion no song, no word
As lovely as her voice, a soft-toned bell
   By wings of nightfall stirred.
Be kind to her, O Lord, and let me keep
   Her hand in mine until the last long sleep.

AT THE SYMPHONY

HOLD now my hand in yours as the baton trembles and rises
As it carves the motionless air, releasing a river of notes
Rushing headlong across the reaches of darkness,
Exploding like flowers of light in our ears, in our throats.

Hold my hand closely as though you were holding the autumn's
first leaf
Warming the cup of your hand with its earliest veins of fire;
Let us not whisper our praise nor turn toward the eyes of each
other,
But over the ripened meadows of memory and desire

Let us run like children on feet that challenge the wind,
Count off the petals of daisies and spread them out in the sun,
Single out a blackberry thicket and taste of its wine's hushed
purple,
Lie down in the grasses of peace till the long green hour is done.

Let us capture this moment completely, call it securely our own,
Flung back into Time, into childhood, walking in sunlight again—
Then when the river of music has spent its last bright torrent,
Bowed with our years, let us go out to the blinding night and
the rain.

BRIGHT HARBOR

I have known harbors at the earth's far rim
Scented with oleanders pale as dawn,
Ports hushed with starlight when the dusk grew dim
And mandolins struck a tune to dream upon.

I have ploughed into the sunset, sails aglow,
Burning with color under the south wind's spell,
Shouted with joy to see the first far row
Of harbor lights, to hear the first faint bell.

I have come home. I bring you lotus flowers,
A shell the sea's wild music burst apart;
I have dropped anchor until my dying hours
Deep, deep within the harbor of your heart.

NO PRIDEFUL THING

No prideful thing it is that it has taken
A world gone under and its breath sucked out,
To lift our eyes toward splendor, to awaken
Our ears again to songs the sparrows shout;

To fall upon our knees and bless the morning,
The air we breathe as flowers breathe the air,
To clasp the wing of Peace, a bright wing burning
Forgotten within our hearts and hold it there.

We were too rich with wine and food and fashion,
Too lustful for the things that matter not,
Too far away from hearthfires, the fierce passion
Of love that saves a nation from its rot.

But since the clock strikes out the hour still,
There yet is time to sow into the sod
The seeds of brotherhood on field and hill,
To turn, through man-made darkness, back to God.

A LETTER FROM THE FRONT

THERE is so much to write, so much of death and dying,
So much of anguish in the dark and stricken mind:
Another city fallen, a shattered fort retaken—
I cannot write for burning eyes growing blind.

But tell me, tell me quickly, swift as lightning,
If summer's on the Georgia fields again,
Crepe myrtle thick with pink and sudden crimson,
Their hot and crinkly blossoms steaming in the rain?

Tell me, tell me if the bleeding hearts of melons
Lie secret-like beneath the ribbons of the corn,
If still, O still the crickets wake the starlight,
The Chattahoochee reddens in the land where I was born?

Still does the quiet duskfall purple up the doorway,
The cotton stretch its acres warm and white;
Is there yet one (O eyes, O lips remembered!)
Who turns and reaches for me in the restless night?

I wait your letters as the dark the sunrise;
There is so little I can ever say—
My words have blood, the smell of death upon them;
Yours, moonlight from a world long centuries away.

SMALL PORTRAIT

HE could have died in war, being young and brave,
Impatient Aprils waiting in his eyes;
Or on some Alpine slope that climbed toward planets,
Or in a jungle's uncharted paradise.

But no. His fate was far less glorious.
Like most of all earth's creatures of distress,
He died of that slow gnawing at the heart,
The dark malignancy of loneliness.

THE LAVENDER LADIES

UNDER their parasols they go
Into the garden, to and fro,
These refugees from love and Time
With sad, slow eyes, words like a rhyme,
Their long years only half concealed
But every heartbreak quite revealed
Beneath the powder that paves their skin.
Poising their teacups brittle-thin,
Their laughter tinkles bright and clear
As prisms in a chandelier.

Pausing beside the flower beds,
Their sighs anoint the poppies' heads,
And as they pass, their lacy frocks
Brush crimson minutes from four o'clocks.
Following them through the drowsy air
Blue eyes of hydrangeas stare and stare.

CHARLESTON

You are an old, old lady by the sea,
With silver hair and cornflower-colored eyes,
A shawl of lavender wrapped carefully
About you. When the last gold daylight dies
And gardenias' breath is burdening the air
Your fingers light bright candles one by one,
And sitting quietly beneath the flare
Of candlelight you see dark shadows run
Across the floor; you read a poem or two,
And breathe the moonlight from your balcony
Turned into lace by shadows cool and blue.
You blow the candles out, and silently
You latch your door and dream as night grows late,
Nor know there is a world beyond your gate.

HOME TOWN

THE town that I am proud to call my own
Is not a lighted city with towers of stone,
No seaport sensuous with the smell of ships.
Yet when the day goes by and darkness slips
Into the hedges and the orchards there,
Of all the world I think my town most fair,
With lamps like casual fireflies in the dark
And lovely as the singing of a lark
The children's voices and the crickets' choir
Lifting toward heaven as the moon lifts higher.
My town lies seldom on a map or chart
Yet bright it twinkles in memory of the heart,
And there I turn, a tired, forgotten man
Deep in the city's blinding, hurrying span,
To claim my peace, my lost identity
Where even the sunflowers' eyes may remember me.

GEORGIA SUMMER

THIS is the spider lily's slumberous hour,
    The gold lantanas on the broken fence,
The cricket's bronze siesta. The cockscomb flower
    Withers and droops in carmine opulence.
Cape jasmines, nodding, shift the last red dust
    A wagon made, and whiten once again;
Spreading hot wings a sparrow eyes the west,
    Scorning its broken promises of rain.
A yellow jacket rises now and falls
    In failing rhythms where the heat drifts clear
Over a motionless sea of cotton bolls
    Ripening on leaves no single wind has stirred.
Red cannas listless tongues hang on the air,
    Speechless, even, for a scarlet word.

OKEFENOKEE SWAMP

HERE is a world which slowed the hands of Time,
Choked back the seasons, the minutes and the hours,
Bound east and west by crocodile and slime,
Northward and southward by cypress and scarlet flowers.

Here thin moons ripen as a lily will
Sheltered by shadows on the blackened glass
Of stagnant waters; slumbering reptiles coil
Where spiders break green backbones of the grass.

There is a music here lost long to man,
And silence past a mortal's heart to know:
Flash of swift wings of fiery color, the span
Of snow-white feathers light as drifting snow.

Yet always fear, fear burning when quiets cease
Over the hyacinths breathing with hesitant breath,
This wild world knowing, as other worlds, that peace
Trembles red-eyed before the claws of death.

SUNDOWN: GEORGIA PLANTATION

THE day is over as surely as the last
Heart-beat that flutters in the breast and dies.
The sweating horses paw the pasture. Fast
The sun's red embers fail. A lone bird cries.
The smell of corn-pone permeates the hour
And pungent coffee boiling in a pot
Sweetens the air like a newly-opened flower;
The day is over, the ripening fields forgot.
A banjo strikes a tune. A lamp, dim-lit,
Throws golden petals of light outside the door
And round the clean-swept steps the toilers sit
Breathing the sunset. Sprawling upon the floor
A young girl ponders on a world that gave
Her feet a path of cotton to the grave.

SONG AT THE MARSHES' EDGE

WHEN the last scythe of darkness bends the grasses
And the slow moon has fled beyond the night,
And the young wind of morning pauses and passes,
Stirring wild lilies cupped with sudden light,

I tread the long lost summers of my mind,
Remember how a lad would take the road
Beside the sunlit marshes, pause to find
A heron's eggs and weigh the fragile load

Within his hands bronzed by a dozen summers,
Ponder on life-to-be and outspread wings,
Then, wading deeply where the berry glimmers
Like rubies over the water where it swings,

Seek other nests and learn the way of birds,
Or wait for hours till a whippoorwill
Breaks the long silence with his grieving words
No man has understood, nor ever will;

And through the long days with his eager eyes
Like cornflowers or the sky, whichever is bluer,
He looked on life, the dream that never dies,
Counted at night a thousand stars, no fewer.

Now still the marsh grows yellow with the morning,
The heron dips into the lighted sky,
His wings and throat with sunrise suddenly burning,
But he is gone, the lad that once was I—

And lonely is my heart, for all that passes
Is fire to keep an old man's heart alight
When the last scythe of darkness bends the grasses
And the slow moon has fled beyond the night.

NEVER THE NIGHTINGALE

NEVER the nightingale shall haunt this marsh
Where the gray herons and the white,
Feathered with moonlight, ride the secret reaches
Of the night.
Never the heartbreak of the nightingale
Shall halt this salty wind—
Only the herons crying, always crying
Brief music pale and thinned,
Shall fly, triumphant, over the making tidals
White and clear
When the slow darkness nibbles at the grasses
Like a young deer.

My heart is long attuned to this wild crying,
The loneliness that stretches like a wave
Where the gray oaks count out the centuries.
I am not brave
Enough to bear a greater burden of beauty
Than these salt marshes bring;
For other men, if there be lovelier lands,
Let nightingales sing.

FOG OFF BRUNSWICK SOUND

LIKE a great seagull lost and flying blind
Fog rides the lower reaches of the sky,
Spreading gray fluttering wings upon the wind,
Dipping into the sea beyond the cry
Of shrimp boats and their masters' hoarsening horn,
Flapping against the brows of fishermen staring
Shoreward with pale salt-weary eyes that burn,
Seeing against the East no promise of clearing.
Blow out, O foghorn, blow! Your plaintive blast
Is not the voice of sea and fog alone—
It is the throat, the cry of all men lost
Deep in the cities' canyons of steel and stone,
On starless deserts or the mountains' height,
Crying forever for a hand, a light.

SEA ISLAND MOONRISE

SCENTED with oleanders' breath
The hesitant darkness falls
Along the leaves still warm with sun.
At slow white intervals
The gulls go by, their sharpened cries
Dividing sky and land,
Then all is darkly one again,
The sky, the tide, the sand.
Only the drowsy grasses stir
Till, bright and suddenly
Like a lone bather, now the moon
Slips in the quiet sea.

FORT FREDERICA

IT is enough that you should leave to us
   This heritage of shattered tabby-stone
Here at the marshes' edges tremulous
   With sandgrass and the herons' wing. Alone,
You rise where rhythmed waters from the sea
   Whisper against your gray and shell-torn walls,
Telling of strange new ships that came to be,
   Of dreams fulfilled. Here, where the sunlight falls
Upon you hidden by honeysuckle flowers,
   A vine of English ivy that knows no death,
We come with but these empty words of ours
   Lost on the air like oleanders' breath,
To speak our gratitude with bended head,
   To say the words that never can be said.

CHRIST CHURCHYARD: ST. SIMON'S

BENEATH this muted conference of oak
Spreading an emerald heaven overhead,
With gray moss hanging like a phantom smoke
Time counts the timeless hours of the dead.
No spoken word awakes the quiet here,
No footfall save the darkness and the dawn,
No stir save jasmine breathing on the air,
Dropping their dying petals on each stone.
Deep in our hearts they sleep, these pioneers,
The young, the brave, the beautiful, the old,
Who made an alien shore so wholly theirs.
Down the slow centuries as the years are told
By Time's cold fingers at his crumbling door
They are at peace with earth. They ask no more.

NOCTURNE: GEORGIA COAST

THE shrimping boats are late today;
The dusk has caught them cold.
Swift darkness gathers up the sun,
And all the beckoning gold
That guides them safely into port
Is lost beneath the tide.
Now the lean moon swings overhead,
And Venus, salty-eyed.

They will be late an hour or more,
The fishermen, blaming dark's
Swift mischief or the stubborn sea,
But as their lanterns' sparks
Ride shoreward at the foam's white rim,
Until they reach the pier
I cannot say if their catch is shrimp,
Or fireflies burning clear.

BAYOU COUNTRY

THIS wild and tangled undergrowth, this dark
Unmoving reach of stagnant waters here
Are all this silent country claims of earth.
The pale blue eyes of water hyacinths stare

Unblinking toward the sky, the heavy breath
Of hot and yellow honeysuckle drifts
Into the dusty lairs of lizard and frog;
Unheralded, the red marsh lily lifts

Its trumpet to a wind that never comes.
From grass to grass the measured silences creep
With guarded step lest they awaken Time
Coiled like a cottonmouth, and fast asleep.

DARIEN

STILL does the sharp sweet smell of Georgia pine
Drift over the river idling to the sea,
But tangled with Queen Anne's lace and trumpet vine
The river front is quiet with memory.
Once deep-hulled vessels leaned against the pier
And sweating Negroes with music on their lips
Loaded the cargoes out, the sunlit air
Glamorous with the smell and beauty of ships.
Here went proud clippers to the far world lying
Beneath a red moon bleeding against the dark,
Freighters and schooners followed by the flying
Of swirling gulls. Now fireflies, spark by spark,
Light up the harbor where only silence stirs,
And Darien weeps for glory that was hers.

THE CAPTIVE

THERE is no turning back for him who goes
Down to the sea at seventeen or so;
The music of the sea that leaps and flows
In changing tides will haunt him; he will go
Forever with the sunrise on his lips,
The purple dusk upon his brow, his ears
Throbbing with cries of gulls above the ships;
He will be a prisoner all his years.
Though full-blown moons may call and he will yearn
For young breasts pale as lotus flowers are,
He must go on where darkening breakers turn
To silver fire beneath the Northern star.
Though he will beat on rocks eternally,
Forever he is captive of the sea.

NOW SINCE THE BLUE PACIFIC

Now since the blue Pacific stretches west,
The gray Atlantic thunders toward the east,
And I am twenty-one and more, and blest
With silver coins of Time to spend, I feast
My eyes upon the maps of all the world:
Where shall I venture when the dawn is red—
To some far jungle where green leaves are curled
By steaming suns till night brings stars and shade?
To high Sierras like a dream of peace
Against a sky so still that no cloud moves,
To lakes that hold a moon without release,
Where nightingales haunt dead men and their loves?
I ponder this, yet knowing well and clear
A single word might hold me captive here.

THE OPEN SEA

THE open sea spreads far and wide
Beyond the reaches of the tide,
Past the farthest harbor light
Rises, plunges, toward the night.

The wind is up, the mast, the sail
Ride against its splitting wail,
And suddenly now my eyes grow blind
With sea ahead, the land behind.

And all I know is what has been,
The port ahead; what rests between
The wave of life, the wave of death,
Lies in the margin of a breath.

A SHIP FOR SINGAPORE

A ship is sailing for Singapore!
   O heart be swift and latch the door!

My fire burns bright and the shadows fall
   In yellow rhythms along the wall.
My love sleeps near and her dreams are deep,
   Her lips a rose that has fallen asleep.
The fire burns bright and the candles glow,
   And I must not go—I must not go!

There is no peace I can know tonight
   Though my love sleeps near and the fire burns bright,
For stars will call from an Indian sky
   And a gold moon haunt me blowing by.
The sea's wild horses will leap and fly,
   Foam on their manes and wind in their eye.

O heart be swift and latch the door—
   A ship is sailing for Singapore!

HOME WITH THE EVENING TIDE

HOME with the evening tide they came,
Shadowy boats of the fishermen
Dragging behind their nets the sun
Till the sea ran copper with its flame.

Purpling, the wharves leaned toward the night
That curved in slowly as a gull.
Above the boats, and beautiful,
Proud Venus kindled a yellow light.

Their nets spread out, the boats safe-tied,
Each fisherman sought a familiar door
Where he would be lost to the sea's wild roar
When love's hand latched the world outside.

A SONG OF LITTLE MEN

THIS is a song of little men,
Of little men who go
From dawn to dusk, or dusk to dawn
With voices meek and slow;
Whose footsteps never carry them
Beyond a gate, a town,
No higher than the nearest hill
And then as swiftly down.

This is a song of men who turn
To little hearths at night
And read of wars, of kingdoms gone,
Of despots and their might,
Who bind their little world with love
And find within its eyes
The light of stars and meteors,
The dream that never dies.

Sing out your songs of proud and brave,
Of generals and kings;
Their day is brief as thistlebloom,
Their flight like sudden wings.
This is a song of little men
Whose strength is iron and leather,
Who have no time for gold nor fame,
Holding a world together.

LAND OF THE WILD SCRUB PINE

THESE are my acres no man can take from me:
Land of the wild scrub pine and herons' flight,
Islands of amethyst hyacinths drifting to sea,
Mornings sun-blinded, hours of breathless night
Waiting the tide, like a great lover, to turn
Shoreward again with starlight in its eyes;
This is the land for which I begin to yearn
When I am no farther away than the gull flies.
There is no gold nor silver in the veins
Of this, my land, but beauty journeys deep
In its black soil to light the tangled skeins
Of spider lily blossoms pale as sleep,
And in the eyes of its people, happy and free,
Burns all the slow wisdom of eternity.

THE SEA IS OLD

WHEN I am broken by the day's long flight
Catching me like a leaf into the wind,
And I drop weary by my bed at night
Too tired for any thought to tread the mind,
I hear, far off, and half a world away
The tireless tides older than centuries are,
The swift white lifting music of the spray
Spending its magic past the farthest star.
The sea is old, the sea is tired, and yet
No dearth of patterns gather, breaking clear
As molten moonlight when the dark has set;
No lessening of music do I hear.
Teach me, O sea, the secret that is yours—
How still, in weariness, the spirit soars.

ISLAND FISHERMEN: ST. SIMON'S

WITH sunset now and ripening of the tide,
The bright day's catch a thing for memory,
Fishermen bronze as nets the sun has dried
Turn to a smaller doorway than the sea,
Taking the dim streets in a motley crowd,
Their salty words and laughter lifting higher,
Leaving the gulls behind them in a cloud,
The small boats rocking, arguing with the pier.
Deserted and forgotten now with night
The boats grow lonely like old fishermen
Knowing no voice, no flare of cigarette
To break the darkness settling warm and plain,
Only the echo of a wave's far roar,
A pale wind breathing silver to the shore.

GEORGIA TOWNS

DEEP in the Georgia night when all
The crickets have hushed their notes
And silence lies upon the needles
Of pines and on the feathered throats
Of sparrows in the star-still boughs,
Across the meadows of my mind
There drift the names of Georgia towns
Softly and slowly as summer wind.

O little half-hid towns I love;
I hear them waking, and in sleep,
And all the music of their names
Like opening flowers, a tidal sweep,
Rests on my heart the hand of peace.
O little towns how close you lie
Upon the warm red clay, how near
Your sun-drenched rooftops touch the sky!
Not all the violins in the world,
The flutes, nor ivory keys
Could take me so triumphantly
And give my soul release.

O Dewy Rose and Talking Rock,
O rain-wet Rising Fawn,
Social Circle where the hand

Of friendship greets the dawn,
O Cave Spring cool as lilies are,
Ty, Ty, Ringgold, Summerville
Where honeysuckle haunts the air
When dusk falls blue and chill—
O Blue Ridge resting like a cloud,
Benevolence and Kennesaw,
Hiwassee, Lovelace, Darien
Where four o'clocks are law,
O Daisytown and Shady Dale,
Across my heart you go
With all a June day's fiery breath,
The grace of winter's snow.

Deep in my last dark Georgia night
When I have come to rest,
Am one again with her red clay hills,
May all the names I love the best
Drift back, in music, over me,
May each come ringing like a rhyme
For one who loves each door, each lane,
An old man losing sleep and Time.

SAILBOAT AT SUNSET

INTO the harbor now she comes
    Through a blue dusk the color of plums,
Dragging a sun pomegranate-red.
    Let now no mortal word be said
Lest the spell break, the silence die
    Pierced by the arrow of a cry.

This is her hour: a ship alone,
    The sea behind. Her anchor down,
Let her sails fold into the night,
    Her bateau ride the waters light
Stirring the moment, pushing to shore
    With only the weeping of an oar.

LILACS

Whatever has happened to lilacs?
I do not see them anymore
Purpling a florist's doorway
Or the bins of a sidewalk store.

I find the bright bells of the tulips,
The red and the gold of the rose,
The honest eyes of daisies
In every garden-close,

But never the lilacs come again
To cities where I must stay.
Perhaps they cling to the countrysides
Of my long lost childhood's day,

Perfuming the windows of the wind
Sun-hot or by rainfall kissed.
Whatever has happened to lilacs,
Or did they ever exist?

SONNET OF NIGHTFALL

ALWAYS I shall remember how the night
Comes on a garden. There can never be
A silence deeper than the day's last light
Brings to a closing petal. Sleepily
A tulip yawns and nods upon the wind,
A bluebell tinkles faintly; four o'clocks
Forget that Time beats on eternally,
Folded in crimson slumber. Hollyhocks
Breathe delicately as music that is thinned
To memory; a bee sways on the stocks
Where shadows hide his golden piracy.
The moon lifts slowly, and its white hand rocks
The gate until the last bright firefly goes
Into the dark cathedral of a rose.

THE TROUT STREAM

ON a day that was pink and yellow,
Pink where the laurel grew,
Dragging the stream with its blossoms,
Shaking it off like dew
Where the wind caught up its branches,
On a day that was yellow with sun
Gilding the foam going over
The falls where the speckled trout run,
I stood on the banks for an hour,
My thoughts as cool as the fern
As I saw a fisherman casting,
As I watched him twist and turn
Deep in the rushing of waters
That carried the sun on its way
Over the rocks and past the laurel,
Bursting in golden spray.

"How beautiful here," I whispered
Quite to myself as I stood
At the edge of the stream's wild music
That woke the quiet wood,
"How at peace the cedars and mountains,"
I added to what I had said,
But a shout in the bright waters shook me
And suddenly I turned my head

To see in the warm yellow morning,
Like an arrow suspended in flight,
A trout with a rhythm like music.
Lovely it was in the light
Of a day that was pink and yellow,
A peaceful day I had thought,
And my heart leaped up as I watched it
Fighting the line that had caught
It up and over the falling
Of waters that were its home,
Up from the banks of the laurel,
Over the spending of foam.

Then I turned away from the fern banks
And I took the valley road,
And when the hours had sifted their sands
And weariness heavied my load,
I paused in a cooling patch of shade
And cursed with an honest breath
That a pink and yellow morning
Should know the silver twitch of death.

IRIS ARE NOT FOR CHILDREN

Iris are not for children laughing, playing,
Nor jonquils with their cups of yellow fire;
These colors belong to April and the old
Whose veins no longer blossom with desire,
Whose years are measured out like raindrops dripping
Slower and slower from a spring's green briar.

Leave summer's roses to the children's fingers,
The scent of lilies through the August night;
They are concerned with these far more than April
For summer is the season of delight
When meadows ripen and a bluebird's pattern
Shadows a sea of daisies hot and white.

Iris are not for children, nor the jonquils.
On any day in Spring you may see the old
Clasping at these first flowers as though they held
The last lone fragment of April they shall hold,
And in their eyes, somehow, a dream that takes them
Across the street and through the wind and cold.

THE DAISY

THE daisy, being what it is,
Affords a lesson none can miss:

Starkly simple, simply white,
A naked heart of yellow light

Beside a wind-swept country lane,
Its head held high in sun or rain,

As bright in April as July,
Oblivious to passersby,

Deaf alike to scorn or praise,
Innocence within its gaze.

Consider how its petals are
Star-shaped and yet it is no star

Though well it might bear such pretense
Or lift in cool indifference

Above each common bloom that blows,
Nod with the aster or the rose,

It draws its wisdom from deep wells:
To be itself and nothing else.

A GRAVE IN BELLEAU WOOD

Jean Gavreau (1902-1917)

Another spring has broken where you lie
Lost deep in slumber and indifferent
To this, or any spring's green ecstasy.
Slowly and silently every leaf is bent
Upward and shining toward its ultimate bloom;
A bird sings in a resurrected tree;
Bright-throated, almost drunk with lilacs' perfume
He sings of spring, of spring eternally.
But what can spring or words of mortals mean
To you who lie one with the springs long lost—
One with the leaves of summer, with the lean
Broken and barren boughs hidden by frost—
To you who gave upon these fields of death
At youth's full tide your last sweet spark of breath?

Ah, what a little, little cross to hold
Above this dust your sacrifice, to mark
The unspent moons, the loves foresworn, the bold
High-singing heart you tossed into the dark!
Only the wind remembers where you lie,
Only the wind, this cross, and one lone bird
Brushing his wing along the quiet sky,
Singing of spring as though you waked and heard.

Ah gallant youth, lost in your loneliness
Save for the wind, this cross—too well, too well
I see the battles' glamour, the laurel's caress
Upon your silent brow, and like a bell
That will not ring, I hear Fame's trumpets blow!
I leave you to your victory, Jean Gavreau.

BEAUTY

No man has set his foot on any land
   But beauty's steps have long preceded him,
Nor climbed a mountain but her steady hand
   Has spread a cloud upon its highest rim.
There is no burning desert man has taken
   Seeking the bones of men who have gone before,
But to some far oasis his eyes awaken
   Discovering her earlier signature.
Always a man must follow, like sparrows' winging,
   The wild, clear winds of beauty down the earth,
Find his own song an echo of her singing,
   His laughter but a pattern of her mirth—
Find even upon the lips of love each day
   The light of dawn that he must kiss away.

INSCRIPTION FOR A SUNDIAL

SENSELESS with beauty pressing like a flame
Around me in this sunlit garden-close—
Blue of the larkspur, yellow of the rose,
White lilies holier than any name—
What can I be that I have earned a place
Where tulips ring their gold cathedral bell,
Where poppies lean upon the air and tell
Their scarlet secrets with an upturned face?
What right have I to know the touch of things
Intangible as wind and shadows' wings,
Things that can never know there is an hour,
A day, a year, only eternity;
O what am I to stand here patiently
And count away the heartbeats of a flower?

AUTUMN

BELOVÉD, Autumn tells us all we know
And all that we shall ever know. Your hand
In mine, this hillside scarlet with the glow
Of orchards ripening on a ripening land,
No word I speak to measure out my love
Avails me anything, nor lip to lip
No kiss, no whisper here shall ever prove
A thing beyond these tremulous leaves that drip
In yellow silence down the listening day.
Once April, like the youth we know this hour
Lay on these boughs, and blooms in bright array;
Now fruit, unbroken promise of the flower,
Drops and is done where stubbled grasses drowse.
All life, all love, is written in these boughs.

PORTRAIT IN SUNLIGHT

WITHIN her garden now she sits and suns,
Her life being over as surely as the last
Death rattle of the rusted Confederate guns.
Oblivious to Time, or traffic past
Her boxwood hedge, she knits away the hours;
A robin twitters and with questioning eyes
Observes her from the pear tree's greening towers
That tremble with his casual melodies.
The village clock speaks with authority,
Dividing afternoon with impartial hands;
She does not hear, nor notice a butterfly
Whose wings reflect the colors of her strands.
She knits, and suddenly smiles, as though a wind
Had stirred the secret lilacs of her mind.

ORCHARD SKIES

I have known skies where Egypt's burning sands
Gave back more bronze and heat than sunset gave,
From tall Sicilian cliffs watched night's dark hands
Plunge a young moon into the sea's wide grave,
And from the shore of China when desire
Had caught and doomed me like a prisoner,
Watched the slow east burst suddenly into fire
Lighting the day with red and lavender.
These were great skies that I could not behold
More than a miserly moment before they had fled,
But when my orchards shake off winter's cold
I can reach up and touch them where they spread
Bright heavens trembling petal-pale and proud,
And break a bough, and keep it, like a cloud.

WOODS IN WINTER

BARE-BREASTED now and unashamed the wood
Stands cold as stone against the quiet hour.
Small eyes of rabbits, sharp with hunger's search
Kindle brown grasses where the wind has stood
Half frozen through a night of motionless birch.
The imminence of snow, pale flake on flake,
Locked in a cloud withholds its shining power
Which in a moment's space may stir and break.
Not till the snow is gone, the bladed cold,
Shall I return to these stripped woods again;
Walking through silence here I seem to move
In measured quiet among a thousand men
Lashed by the whips of life, broken and old,
Lonely as all men are bereft of love.

SNOW

YOU were so young then, far too young to know
The meaning of snow.
Watching it fall, your face at the pane,
Your breath making there a misty stain,
You turned and looked at me
And suddenly
"Isn't it beautiful falling?" you said.
I smiled and nodded my head.

Wherever you are, a score of winters has passed.
Springs and summers and autumns lie fast
Under the blankets they spread.
I think of you now, your dear dark head
Pressed at the pane, your eyes alight,
Laughing to see a world turned white,
Praying the drift at the door overnight
Would imprison us there. Little you guessed
The cries in the dark. You said they were wind,
Shadows were shadows, not old men thinned
To the shape of their hunger, hiding in wait
For a crust of bread, or a south-bound freight.

You were so young, too young to know.
I think of you now, watching the snow . . .

THE WEATHER

"How is the weather out?" you ask, on rising,
Clapping your hands together before the fire.
I scan the dark barometer, surprising
You with the low degree. "It will work higher,"
You say, "as morning wears." And so it will.
Then, lost in April's quiet you will come
Up from the garden with a daffodil,
Or later on, the pale delphinium
Will fill your hat, larkspur and baby's-breath,
And you will frown and ask me the degree,
And beg a glass of water before your death
From summer's gold and blue humidity.
But never have you asked, in any year,
If weather of the heart be dark or clear.

CALL BACK THE SPRING

WHEN you and I who now are worn with loving
   Deep in these daisies, lost to Time and man,
You who were so afraid of love, of roving
   Too far from where your father's acres ran,
I, fired with youth, who carry on my tongue
   The words of lovers and speak them over again,—
When we are weary and no longer young,
   Are half a world away from where we have lain
This sun-drenched afternoon—shall we not yearn
   Dark in the night, and with a sudden cry
Remember daisies by a hill's sharp turn,
   The lass you were, the lad that once was I,
And, sated with slumber, murmur a half-heard thing
   Beseeching all the gods: Call back the Spring?

MOUNTAINS WILL NEVER KNOW

MOUNTAINS will never know this thing:
The earliest footsteps of the spring.

For spring will seek the valley first
And let it quench a season's thirst
In thawing brooks and leaping streams
Releasing winter's ice-locked dreams;
Here laurel will open startled eyes
At spring's first signal in the skies,
While neighbors run to tell each other
There's been a breaking in the weather.

Mountains will stand steadfast and be
Horizon-high with jealousy.

BLOODROOT

Coming upon it suddenly, unaware,
Finding the star-shaped petals hidden there
Beneath the burnished leaves of autumns lost,
I said: This is a shining star of frost
A leaf has harbored from the early sun,
But going closer, being a curious one,
I stooped and brushed the quiet leaves away
Watching it tremble in the light of day
Even as I, beholding beauty come
Unheralded. In wild delirium
I thought: Now spring has come again to light
The darkened wood with boughs of white,
To blind the eye, to halt the breath,
To shout aloud the lie of death.

But then I said, lest barren boughs should hear,
Quite to myself: This thing is very clear;
I am a trespasser, have come upon
A secret. Being honest, and alone,
I pushed the copper leaves back into place,
Hiding the bloodroot flower's startled face,
Keeping the spring's white secret in my heart
Safely as under the leaves I tore apart.

WITH ALL OUR VANITIES

WITH all our vanities and bright opinions,
Our swiftly flashing tongue and quickening eye,
I wonder if we know that we are lesser
Than any shadow we are measured by?

We polish up dull words until they glitter,
Sharpen our wits like knives and shape our creed,
Yet who amongst us does not cringe, half-frightened,
Hearing a slow breath stirring in a seed?

Wrapped in deep solitudes we fashion motors
Shattering the silence, musical with power,
And yet, where is the wheel that turns, unfolding
A single rose before its scarlet hour?

REMEMBER THEN

IF you should come upon my skeleton
Blanching in marsh or sand
In some far year no calendar now shows,
Pity it not, but touch it with your hand
As you would touch a bird's wing or a rose.

Remember then, in that strange meeting place,
Its walls have harbored well
At their full tide a flood of spring's green days
Fired with the breath of beauty's miracle;
That once, within that emptiness dwelt praise
Of God, of love triumphant no matter how small
The fare it set each hour.
Remember, too, before you turn away
Where loneliness blossoms like a desert flower,
To will me all the peace your lips can say.

AUGUST GARDEN

Here in this darkening garden where you came
In other years, time out of mind almost,
I come tonight. The warm wind speaks your name,
Slow shadows on the trellis like a ghost
Return and cross the grasses and the stones.
The pool, as indolent as Time is now,
Waits for a lone green frog's familiar tones;
Within its mirror stars like fireflies glow.
There is a hint of early autumn here
As dew slides down a canna's pointed spear
Making a small sound silvery and clear.
Cooler the wind comes now; a late bird cries.
I rise and go, to leave the questioning eyes
Of opening moonflowers, having no replies.

SUMMER'S END

THERE is a somber sadness in the going
Of summer's blossoms down the amber wind,
In music of the maple's first leaves blowing
In ranks of scarlet all too suddenly thinned.
It is a time to pause, considering
How lightly, all too lightly, beauty lies
Upon the scales of mortal measuring;
How swiftly beauty comes, how swiftly dies.
Now all that summer leaves is but a stream
Whose mirror bears the memory of her,
A late rose lonely in its languid dream
Beside a lane where only grasses stir,
And lingering at the edges of the day
A sunflower's dial that ticked the summer away.

A SNOW SO WIDE

WHOSE prints these are across the snow
I cannot say; I do not know.
But journeying this path alone
With silence on the heart like stone,
I hope that I can overtake
Him traveling through wind and flake,
A lonely shadow in a night
So brittle that it snaps with white
Where fir and spruce and alder bend
Beneath the fingers of the wind.

I must catch him if I can
And speak a word or two. No man
Has eyes enough to witness all
This blinding rush of petal-fall—
A snow so deep, a snow so wide
It takes a county in its stride,
Making a heaven where none was
Of cattle lanes and meadow grass,
And tell it clearly, eye to eye,
Without his word being called a lie.

I'll need him in a time or two
To bear me out tonight was true:
The smallest flake knowing where to go,
This music of my feet on snow,
And pines and firs along the way
Shining there as proud as day;
Each cabin white and glittering
As if inside there slept a king.
And overhead, through wind and flake,
A word that makes the silence break,
A voice I knew I'd never hear,
But speaking soft and crystal-clear.

DECEMBER NIGHT

THROUGH all this frozen night there is no sound
  Save my white footsteps on a whiter ground,
No stir up from the meadow nor the brake
  Lost in the whitening wind beyond the lake.

How soft the lamps come on, their sudden gold
  Shining from windows warming up the cold;
How pale the trees, how bowed their branches down
  With loveliness one cannot see in town.

But hush, and listen! Above this stretch of white,
  This swirl of snow that blinds me like a light
I hear a slow sound plain and high and far—
  The wind's cold fingers polishing a star.

A DAISY'S EYE

ALWAYS in summertime I wish that I
Might stare astonished as a daisy's eye
That looks on every dawn as though it were
The eastern sky's first lanterned traveler,
And at the sun of noon burning molten-bright
As though it were the earth's last show of light.

There is no thing on earth but it is new
To any daisy's eye: the fleeting blue
Of butterfly wings, the sudden golden drone
A bee composes over the scented cone
Of clover blossoms; the repeated sight
Of daylight going, or the coming night.
The first crust of a new moon, or the last,
Alerts a daisy's eye and holds it fast.

Always in summertime I wish that I
Might stare astonished as a daisy's eye
At everything I've seen before, and find
A newness and a brightness that would blind
Me to my way of thinking, and hold my tongue.
A daisy's eye might keep an old man young.

SUMMER SHALL COME AGAIN

SUMMER shall come again, her slender rose
Lend its bright ruby to the wind's blue hand,
And over meadows where the clover blows
Bronze orchestras of bees awake the land.
Small streams shall speak their music to the sun
And in the green cathedrals of the trees
The robins stare at summer till summer is done
And all her splendor ravels to memories.
Summer shall come again, and in due time,
But in my heart no more her sun will climb
Nor any flower unfold its miracle,
For she is gone whose laughter was a bell,
Whose love made bread and wine of every stone
And kindled stars and moons when there were none.

SO BRIEF A THING

So brief a thing is beauty, hold it close,
As closely as your heart would hold a wing
That soon is flown again, unraveling
Its splendor down the lyric way it goes.
Drink sunsets deeply; drink their dregs of rose
That linger in the darkening sky. A thing
Of beauty is a glory that will sing
Its way into your soul. Your blood that flows
Will quicken into music in your veins.
Look long upon all beauty that you see—
Hushed lavender of lilacs and a tree
Armored in sudden silver of the rains.
Hold beauty closely; never let it go
Till eyes are blind and lips are pale as snow.

THE RIVER BOATS

WHERE are the old side-wheelers now,
The river boats of yesteryear—
The *Comet* and *Vesuvius*
Whose whistles sharp and clear
Routed a parish from its bed,
Shaking the morning air?

(Sing low, O voices from the past—
Breathe deep O honeysuckle flower!)

Where is the shining *Prince of Wales*,
The *Washington* and *Southern Belle*,
The *Sea Gull* and the *Unicorn*
That made the Mississippi swell
In bright, swift tides against the wharves?
Where are they now? Who can tell?

(Play soft, O banjo from the shadows,
Bleed red, O melons on the vine!)

Where does the *Annie Laurie* rest,
The bold *Diana's* fabled hull,
The *Sally Robinson* trail her smoke?
Proud as a lady and beautiful
Casting her shadow in the sun,
Where steams the *Belle Creole?*

(Finger the willows gently, wind,
Spill all your silver, Delta Moon!)

Where are the boats of yesteryear?
It is a secret I cannot keep:
Deep in the harbor of a dream
They drift with tall majestic sweep,
The songs of stevedores long silent,
And all their pilots fast asleep.

THE WHITE CATHEDRAL

DEEP in the winter woods I went
   Alone, O quite alone.
Above me boughs of cedars bent
   Carved and white as stone.

There was no bird in all that wood,
   No grey surprise of hare,
And I could see from where I stood
   No footprint there.

Where morning went I never knew,
   And I could never tell
Which was the path where laurel grew,
   Or birch, or winterbell.

But pausing there, a man half-blind,
   How good it was to know
Wherever I looked that I would find
   Contentment deep as snow,

And hear no word and see no thing
   In all that world of white
To question this pale leveling,
   This shining height.

OCTOBER EVENING

THE pears hang heavy, gold along the day.
Reluctantly the crisp wind-sharpened leaves
Forsake the quivering boughs and drift away,
Lost in the gathering dusk, the wind that grieves.
Chrysanthemums, once red and yellow lights,
Upon the rustling grass lie frozen, brown;
Slow chimney sparks, fireflies of winter nights,
Blossom in yellow patterns and are done.
The year is waning, guttering like a lamp,
Losing itself in darkness and in Time,
One with the tiring wind, the ripened pears.
A late bird, shadow-blinded, fumbling home
Cries loneliness through silence cold and damp;
A whole world answers him, yet no one hears.

BLUE MORNING

As in a dream I saw them, seven children,
The sun of Sicily in their eyes, their laughter
Ringing like bells of foam the wild sea tosses,
Breaking upon a rock grown numb with music.
I watched the wild flowers at their feet bend downward
And up again, when suddenly their feet were gone
Following the hoops they rolled, the ball they threw.
And standing there that blue Sicilian day,
Etna behind me like a shield forever,
Pale almonds over my head in a pink cloud,
I said: O God, that I could mold this moment
Into a stone, a shape and sound and beauty
Imperishable, to press against my heart,
To wear smooth with my fingers when I am old,
For being old is doubting all one saw
And heard, and knew, upon the shores of youth;
Age only believes the harsh wind at the door,
The dying embers, the rattle in the throat. . . .

DARK SONG

O, I shall find it long before I die:
The cure for heartbreak, for these little deaths
I die from day to day in every season.
Like lightning striking swiftly from the sky
I shall discover it before my breath's
Last voyaging. Deep in the veins of reason

There is a cure, I know, for doors that close
Past comprehension, and for words unspoken,
For lips withdrawn and toward another's turning—
But when I find it, to the reddest rose
I shall be blind as night, and lame, and broken;
O God, and yes, past all a mortal's yearning.

THE SKIER

How silently, and with a feather's grace
He takes the blinding slopes of glittering ice,

Now swift, now slow, now curving left or right
Over the reaches of a world turned white,

A sweep, a sigh, a surge of ecstasy,
Downward, and on, a heart set suddenly free,

Leaping and flowing, patterned like a rhyme,
A bird of air, a moment loosed from Time. . . .

WHEN EACH WHITE CLOUD

When each white cloud has reached its destination
Across the cool blue oceans of the sky,
And every rose's crimson conflagration
Of beauty burns to ashes I shall lie
One with the insignificant dust, nor know
In that dark silence how the slow dawns broke
In ripening fires across impatient hills,
Nor how at dusk the ivory moonflowers woke
To claim their little hour. Time will flow
Above me like a wind that stirs and stills
The dust, to still and stir the dust again;
I shall forget all earth, its babbling men,
Remembering only where the dark is deep
That you and I have loved; then I shall sleep.

RETIRED SEA CAPTAIN

WEEP not for him, come home to stare away
The long, slow years that reach beyond the sea,
To add his curious coins of memory,
A Midas from the harbors of his day.
Before the hearthfire he remembers now
Algiers, a million diamonds in the dark,
Proud Istanbul, and Athens white as snow,
Liverpool loud with seagull and the lark.
He nods, and beckons, and Calcutta comes
With all the fires of sunrise in its eyes;
The Congo answers with a tide of drums,
Pale China tells him all her mysteries.
Weep not for him. He rides the sea tonight
Before a hearth where threads of slow flames climb,
His compass trembling toward the north star's light,
Safe in the archipelago of Time.

HARBOR NIGHT

EVEN the gulls grow tired when day is ending
And the young stevedores' last weary cries
Drift over the harbor in forgotten music
And the new tide comes in with quickening sighs.

Eyelids of lanterns like slow fireflies flutter
Along the silent pier, and whippoorwill
From drowsy willow trees across the river
Strike one high note and hold it, stubborn and shrill.

Like an old drunken seaman now the sun
Deserting the harbor pockets his gold and goes
To some far salty tavern beyond the night,
A tavern whose dark address nobody knows.

SAY THAT HE LOVED OLD SHIPS

SAY that he loved old ships; write nothing more
Upon the stone above his resting place;
And they who read will know he loved the roar
Of breakers white as starlight, shadow lace
Of purpling twilights on a quiet sea,
First ridge of daybreaks in a waiting sky,
The wings of gulls that beat eternally
And haunt old harbors with their silver cry.
Speak softly now, his heart has earned its rest,
His heart that knew each alien star by name,
Knew passion of the waves against his breast
When clouds swept down the sea and lightning's flame
Tore skies asunder with swift finger tips.
Write nothing more; say that he loved old ships.

CONFESSION

My heart will never, never be yours alone.
Too many things I love to speak the lie:
Red tides of sunset breaking on the sky,
Slow twilights, and the first rose suddenly blown
To fiery splendor on a day in spring;
Cold mountain water passionate and strong
And wild with music, and the first sharp song
Of birds when day has folded like a wing.
My head will lie upon your shoulder deep
Into the night, and I will find you fair,
And swing the gates to heaven in my sleep
Beside you, breathing the fragrance of your hair,
And though my lips shall always claim your own
My heart will never, never be yours alone.

TO THE YOUNGER GENERATION

THOUGH you will not believe, there was a time
  When summer was a breath across the heart
Of wine-red clover and deep-scented thyme,
  A field where lovers lay and tore apart
A flower's petals, shaped their years to be,
  Stared into stars until the skies were one;
When men turned home with dusk and slumbered free,
  Dreams burning with promise of the morning's sun.
You will not find it now; this is a world
  Of knives thrust deep in every brother's back,
Of flaming cities, madness kindled, hurled
  At sea and jungle with each new attack.
It was not always so, earth battle-scarred.
  Peace once has walked her ways. Believe my word.

THE LAST HOUR

WE are no stronger than the roses are
In that last hour when the hands of Time
Measuring the blood's slow rhythms pause, and chime;
We who are brave and strong, who wear the scar
Of battles that have wrung our wits apart,
We who have breathed as pauper and as king,
Laughing at life and holding each golden thing
More precious than the beating of our heart;
With knowledge like a rudder in the brain
Only in that last hour are we wise,
Weighing each waning breath with pleading eyes,
Knowing the blood's last battle all in vain.
It will not vary under any star:
We are no stronger than the roses are.

A SPANISH TOWN

THERE was a Spanish port I knew
That slumbered in the sun;
Even the mandolins fell asleep
Slowly one by one,
And all the boys whose eyes were lakes
Of midnight in the day,
And all the girls with scarlet lips
Sang afternoons away.

When twilight's petals trembled down
Like dew-wet violets
All the doorways blossomed wide
With lamps and castanets,
And laughter rippled like a bell
Across the happy hour,
Till past the waning of the moon
Night folded like a flower.

O there it was I learned to laugh,
And there I learned to sing,
And all the hours of earth and sea
Breathed deep with miracles of spring.
And bright the blood flowed in my veins
And on my eager lips
The taste of wine burned red and deep
As sunset over ships.

But that was long and long ago.
And though I search tonight
The streets I learned to call by heart
There is no face, no light
To beckon me within a door,
To share a dream, a rhyme.
There is a stranger at my side;
He says his name is Time.

SUNSETS

Sunsets with you were more than suns going down,
Slow darkness settling on the pine and fir,
Warm eyes of every valley's drowsy town
Blinking toward slumber as the late winds stir.

No sun was lost beyond a single hill,
No ridge of reddening fire, no cloud of gold.
Safe in my heart I keep their embers still,
My lantern when the years have made me old.

A SNOWY MORNING

LITTLE he leaves the forest, this young deer
To testify swift beauty traveled here

In measured leaps and morning-lighted eyes.
Only this pattern of his small hooves lies

Imprinted starlike in the deepening snow
Under the crystal branches swinging low.

Little it is to mark his lyric way
Over the long drifts of the frozen day,

Yet somewhere in the annals of Time's cold pen
I know of lesser pathways left by men.

WILD FLOWERS

I have known wild flowers in the fields of Spain
Slumberous, hot with sunlight, scarlet as fire,
And walking past them I have hushed my voice
Lest it should wake them from their languid hour.
Yellow some were, and blue as were those skies
Where no cloud foamed across their breathless space,
But none among them slumbering in the sun
Held half the brightness, the color of your eyes.

And on a cliff that looked upon the sea,
A tall Sicilian cliff that knew no pattern,
I came upon a fragrance unaware—
Flowers that seemed to plunge into the waters
Drunk with a beauty that was theirs alone;
But no, not there, not even there nor since
Has bloomed a wild flower sweeter than your lips.

ONCE MORE THE TIDE

ONCE more into the tide, O love, once more
To feel the lifting spray, the amber air,
Ranges of foaming mountains breaking clear,
Their sun-hot music thundering to the shore.
Once more to find a singing shell or two,
The starlike printings of the sandpipers' feet
Scudding along the shore; suddenly the sweet
Breath of the sandflowers blinking wide eyes of blue.
These are the quickening hours our hearts must know;
Not the long years for us. Briefly, and only,
Love blossoms and dies. I swear these words are so
By all the broken and old, the weary, the lonely.
Once more the tide, O love, the lifting spray
Before the long winter breaks upon the sea.

THE PEAR TREE

THERE was a pear tree that I used to climb
   When I was young the sunnier side of Time,
A tree that always pointed up to where
   The sky was bluer, with cloud galleons there,
And in its branches, white, and later green,
   I watched the small fruit shaping in between
The pointed leaves that fluttered in the wind
   And made a sort of music warm and thinned.
I dared the highest branches, being small,
   Knowing not again would I ever stand so tall.
Since that was all a surge of Time away
   I never go back to the tree where I used to play.
It may be gone, like childhood. And the eye
   Is never so kind to men as memory
That lets my pear tree blossom April-white
   Again, again, even on this winter night.

ENDINGS

ALWAYS an ending. Shall I never see
Some glory hidden from the slow sure blade
Beneath whose sharpened edge all things are laid,
All beauty and all love? Can there not be
Some rose that blooms beyond its farthest reach,
A sun that will not leave the blue bright day,
A meadow flower that will not shatter away,
Some wave that is not lost upon the beach?
I fill my eyes with dawn; I drink it deep,
And day is lost to dusk, and dusk to night;
I watch the moon; it blinds me, and I weep
To see it waning like a weary light.
O earth, O sky, O sea! Tell me these lies:
Beauty lives always—and love never dies!